"Real patriotism is being committed to the Constitution, not to a political party or personal belief." – Marcus D. Johnson

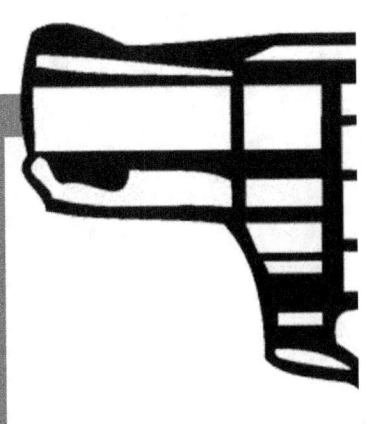

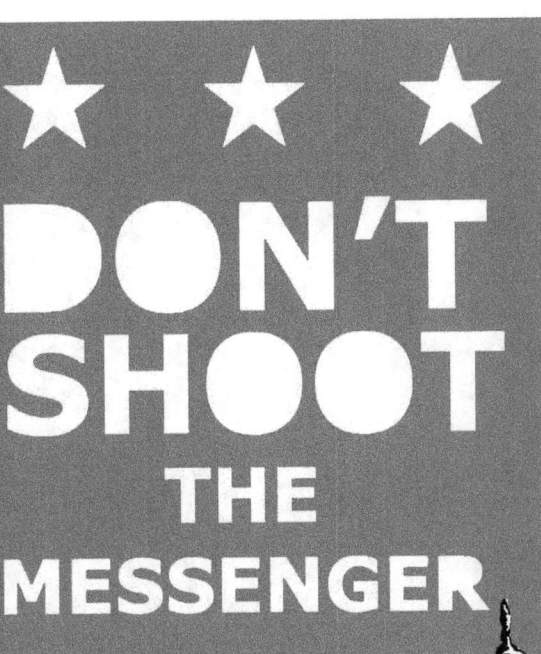

DON'T SHOOT THE MESSENGER

Table of Content

DON'T SHOOT THE MESSENGER

"Message to America, the Democrats, Republicans, Conservatives, Liberals, The Far-Left, The Alt-Right, Blue Lives Matter, Black Lives Matter, All Lives Matter, Islamophobics, Christians, Racists, Super Americans, the Mainstream Media, and the Justice System."

By Marcus D. Johnson

Message to America

Undoubtedly America has had its fair share of con men. From William Rockefeller Sr., to Charles Ponzi, to Bernie Madoff, and now arguably the one man I consider to be the master of deception, misdirection, and Grand Puba of the confidence game – Donald J. Trump.

By now, we can safely assume that the 2016 election will either be one of the most talked about scandals or one of the most studied cases of corruption in history. *(Or maybe it will be that one section in the history books of our children's children where all the pages are just glued together.)*

Truth is - the 2016 election showed both the Democrats and the Republicans true colors - the lack of leadership and the political crabs in a bucket-like mentality. However, in the end, Americans were left to pick what some people called the lesser of two evils. But let's be real about it, even though the Democrats played themselves by outing Bernie Sanders –Americans did their part and Hillary Clinton won the popular vote (*by over 2 million votes*). Democrats however, allowed the loophole known as the Electoral College to be exploited either by the Republican Party or by the Russians.

Truth is, it could've been avoided.

Flashback to the 2000 election (Bush vs. Gore) when the Democrats won the popular vote but lost the election due to the Electoral College. Now fast forward 16 years later and here we go again. Even though the 2000 election had its own cloud of conspiracy hovering around it, in the end the Electoral College pulled the same move to steal the 2016 election – ultimately handing over our country to a lying tyrant.

It doesn't matter if it was Russian intervention or not – ultimately, the 2016 election came down to the Electoral College (Which was created in retrospect to combat the high population of southern states that own slaves. And truthfully it doesn't serve any purpose to the American people of the 21st Century).

Let's keep it real, the Democrats got hoodwinked in 2000. However, in 2004 Bush won the popular vote and the Electoral College, which solidified his 2nd term as president. And with Barack Obama winning both the popular vote and Electoral College in 2008 and 2012, no one really cared about the irrelevancy of the Electoral College.

The reality is, the Democrats sat around on their thumbs for 16 years and the same irrelevant loophole (*known as the Electoral College*) came back to bite them in the ass, AGAIN.

Now with Trump as president, and not only are some Americans questioning our democratic process but other countries and nations are questioning the competence

of Americans as a whole.

Trump was at least half right about one thing – they're

laughing, but not at us – at him.

Message to the Democrats

Hip Hop Artists and Celebrities

The 2008 election seemed like it was the year of the socially conscious celebrity, especially in the Hip Hop industry. But like everything else in the industry - it was a fad, a trend, or tool like Snapchat – just something artists and celebrities used to expand their fan base.

Let's be real, the 2008 presidential elections had A, B, and even D list celebrities jumping on the Obama band wagon. And it worked. The proof was in the numbers – Hip Hop artists and celebrities along with the star power they brought to the 2008 elections helped elect the first black President of the United States of America.

Undeniably, this was the most historical moment in American history and it seemed like every artist and celebrity wanted to be a part of it. Unfortunately, when it came to the 2016 election, undeniably another important election in American history, CRICKETS, no one was speaking up or speaking out...

It wasn't until election night when everyone *thought* it was time to throw a victory party, that's when artists and celebrities finally decided to jump onboard but they were sadly mistaken. Trump won.

Hillary won the popular vote, that's a fact, but overall she still lacked the social popularity needed to secure a solid victory. Let's be honest, Hillary had minimal support from the Hip Hop community compared to President Obama. Even if Hillary wasn't your first choice because of the mass incarceration attached to the Clinton name or maybe you preferred Bernie Sanders, reality is – besides Killer Mike – there was no other artist or celebrity actively speaking up or speaking out during the 2016 election like there was in the 2008 and the 2012 elections.

Where were all those artists and celebrities from 2008 and 2012 that basically hit the campaign trail screaming "Hope!", "Change!", and "Yes We Can!"? What happen to Vote or Die, Rock the Vote, and Respect My Vote? Where were all those artists and celebrities that rode the Obama coattail to victory? Because from where I'm standing, in 2016 they all failed - epically.

That resulted in leaving millions of their fans and followers receiving fraudulent news, being misrepresented by sources that don't share their best interest, and sometimes not being represented at all. And I understand it's not your responsibility to report the news, however it is your responsibility to represent your culture, and you do have some responsibility to use your platform for more than just monetary gain.

Understand black communities were being painted as war zones. Our youth was being painted as "Super Predators" and the Republicans were able to scoop up a hand full of *House Negros* and low level con men to run around the country and preach their lies. Sad thing is moguls of the industries sat idle and watched people like Sheriff David Clarke Jr., Pastor Mark Burns, Pastor

Steve Parson, or Rev. Darrell Scott persecute the black communities by painting an unrealistic reality while trying to further their own political agendas. In my opinion, none of these individuals represented the best interests of the black community. However, instead of the black community picking its own voices to represent them, Republicans picked the voices that dominated the media. And those artists and celebrities who have a platform, had the ears of millions, and were politically active in the 2008 and 2012 elections – they all just stood by and said nothing in 2016.

Women and the Working Class

Hillary basically won the black vote by default, mostly because the majority of people weren't going to vote for Trump period, or maybe because they just liked her husband. No matter how you add up the votes, two votes were missing - the Women vote and the vote from the Working Class. And it seemed like no matter how much women hated Trump for some of the things he said and allegedly done, for some reason they despised Hillary even more than Trump. Either they didn't approve of her choice to stand by her husband throughout his infidelities or maybe they felt like she verbally attacked his alleged victims. But believe it or not, 96 years after The Women's Bureau of the Department of Labor was formed, there are women who still think the job of President of the United States is a job more suited for a man. But in my opinion, she failed to speak to the heart of what people cared about the most: money, jobs, and work.

Think about it, Trump had his fair share of sexual scandals to fight too. He did what all con men do – boast unrealistic gains and claim outrageous returns. Trump talked about job creation and so called winning so much that it drowned out the all the sexual accusations, scandals, and hate filled speeches. On the other hand, Hillary didn't talk about job creation enough; she should've been screaming "YOU GET A JOB, YOU GET A JOB, and YOU GET A JOB!" like she was on an episode of Oprah Favs. Because the reality was no matter how detailed her job creation plan might have been, NO ONE KNEW ABOUT IT.

Let's keep it real. Trump didn't have a real job creation plan then and still doesn't have a real job creation plan now. Honestly, Trump can tell his supporters anything as long as he says it's going to create jobs. And when it came to the working class, Trump appealed to the pockets of some and the greed of others. While Hillary was trying to appeal to the minds of some and hearts of others - which in my opinion was the wrong plan altogether.

Understand this country is more than 60% white, and even though the overall country's unemployment rate was down, that still left a large amount of willing and ready white men and women out of work.

And the reality is, Hillary either didn't understand that Americans were ready to get back to work or she didn't know how to tap into that American desire to be an industrial force again.

And that cost her votes and maybe the election.

Message to the Republicans

Since 2010 the Republican Party has been weak, pissed, and scrambling for stability. That same year Republican Senate Minority Leader Mitch McConnell made a public statement saying *"The single most important thing we want to achieve is for President Obama to be a one-term president."* Even though this didn't happen and President Obama was elected for a second term, it was a warning shot directed at the Democrats. The gloves were off and the Republican Party was ready and willing to play dirty. And like the saying goes *"The enemy of my enemy is my friend"*. However, no one ever tells you that *"The enemy of your enemy, might be your enemy too"*, and Trump was the enemy that took the Republican Party off guard.

Let's face it – Trump isn't a Republican or a Democrat.

He's a con man that bullied his way into the Republican

Party and now the country is being run by a political

idiot. But who can blame him, The Republican Party

was divided and a house divided cannot stand.

However, with all of the confusion it just made it easier

for Trump to systematically attack everyone in the

Republican Party that was his opposition or anyone who

opposed his views. And like a classroom bully – he

attacked them, not with logic but by making jokes.

Except Trump wasn't making jokes, he was actually

making false accusations. Honestly, the Republicans

allowed Trump to mind fuck them, walk in to their house,

and take the keys. No matter if it was by choice or by

force. But from the outside looking in, it looked like the

Republicans threw the fight against a man that is

nowhere near as politically minded as they are. And with over 20+ years of political experience amongst the Republicans candidates alone, there is no reason why they couldn't work together long enough to block the nomination of a habitual liar, with countless scandals, numerous sexual allegations, who was spreading hate and division, on top of intentionally not disclosing his tax returns.

Honestly right now, the only thing Republicans can to do is work with together alongside the Democrats to get Trump out of office. Then they need to figure out how they let this happen so it won't ever happen again.

Message to the Libertarian and Green Party

If you plan on making any type of move – the time is now. The Democrats are still licking their wounds from the election, the Republicans are still shell shocked from the mind fucking Trump gave them, and Jill Stein made a big impact on the 2016 election. Big enough to let Americans know that they have a third party option other than Democrat or Republican.

The most important thing now is staying relevant, because out of sight, out of mind.

Whoever the party leaders are, they need to make some political noise. They need to deploy strong political minds that are ready to kick ass and take names. If you ask some people, both the Republicans and the Democrats have been allowed to get away with what some would consider crooked, murderous, or just flat out treasonous activity.

I know it's dirty to kick your enemy while they're down, but they're not down, they're just distracted.

Let's keep it real, the Trump administration is under a lot of scrutiny right now because of all the lies and ties to Russia. The Democratic Party is on the attack against Trump to regain some respect for stabbing Bernie Sanders in the back and the Republican Party is still shell shocked from the mind fucking Trump gave them.

So this is the time to pass policies. And even if you can't get a single policy passed, you're making noise and staying relevant in the eyes of your supporters and in the eyes of anyone who didn't know you even existed.

And again, the most important thing now is staying relevant.

Understand grassroots movements are powerful and the Women's March is a perfect example of just how powerful a movement can be. Realistically speaking, that one march rallied so many supporters that it dwarfed the attendance of Trumps own inauguration from the previous day. Not to mention the protest against Trump's illegal travel ban, the protest against

Trump Care, and even the Tax Day marches were all proof that grassroots movements work.

However, the only objective from this point on should be to stay relevant, not be ignored, overlooked, or overrun.

Message to the Liberals and Conservatives

Understand that you are an American first and a

Conservative or Liberal second. However, now a days,

people throw around the titles of Conservative and

Liberal like it's some kind of insult or claim it like it's

some type of badge of honor. And in most cases, one

will claim that the other is un-American or less patriotic

because they don't share the same views.

In my opinion, many of them don't understand what

being a real American is or what real patriotism is.

Real patriotism is being committed to the Constitution,

not to a political party or personal belief. Real patriotism is supporting legitimate legislation, legitimate policies, and not just supporting politicians.

So it doesn't matter if you are Conservative or Liberal – it's un-American and unpatriotic to support unconstitutional laws, policies, and legislation. It's un-American and unpatriotic to put your personal beliefs, your personal views, and a political party above the Constitution.

Message to Christians, Racists, Islamophobics, The Far-Left, and The Alt-Right

To address Christianity - the religion as a whole - does not serve Christians justice. Truth is that some people don't understand there's a difference between being a Christian and being Christ-like. At first glance, you wouldn't know America is a country built on freedom of religion and the separation of church and state. That's because politicians peddle religion, mainly Christianity to Americans like it's written into the Constitution; shit, some people act like if you're not Christian - you're not American or at least not American enough.

Look around you, America is a melting pot of people, religions, cultures - you know the saying, "land of the free, home of the brave". More like – land of the greed, home of the slave. Let's just be real about it, this country was built on racial diversity and on the backs of free and/or cheap labor. Call them Christians, Slave Masters, or Businessmen - no matter how you look at it, people of color have always been the victims of oppression in this country. It started the moment Europeans stepped foot off the first boat and nearly extinguished the "AMERICAN" Indians. Add in the 400+ years of slavery, the 1939 Japanese Internment Camps, Latinos & Mexicans *allegedly* stealing jobs, now everyone seems to be suffering from Islamophobia since 9/11. Seems like everyone is totally ignoring or disregarding the countless Christian terror attacks that happen in this very same country.

Wade Michael Page, Scott Roeder, Jim David Adkisson, Paul Jennings Hill, Eric Rudolph, James Charles Kopp, John C. Salvi, David Lane, Bruce Pierce, Timothy McVeigh, Dylan Roof, and Joseph Stack were all white American Christian men who committed acts of terrorism in and against the United States.

Joseph Stack even carried out a suicide attack on the IRS building in Austin, Texas, by flying a plane into it. But if you let the government and mainstream media tell it – they were all lone wolfs or mentally disturbed. On the other hand, nearly every person of color or a person with 2nd, 3rd, or even 4th generation ties outside the United States is connected to ISIS. For example, even though the two Boston bombers Dzhokhar Anzorovich Tsarnaev and Tamerlan Anzorovich Tsarnaev were originally from Russia, but somehow the government and mainstream media managed to connect them to ISIS and radical Islam. News Flash - there were far more terrorist attacks committed on America soil by white far right extremists and white radical Christians than this country will ever admit. It's just easier to accuse a nonwhite, non-American, whose beliefs are slightly different than yours.

Fact is - this country is littered with radical Christian groups who spread hate speech, religious propaganda, and commit acts of violence in the name of God. Shit, the Ku Klux Klan is a religious terrorist organization built on hate and violence. They burned crosses in front of homes, bombed businesses, burned down churches, and murdered people that worshipped the same God they worshipped.

And none of those actions or the actions of radical Christian groups today resemble anything close to Christ-like or the message of peace that was preached by Jesus.

Message to Black Lives Matter and All Lives Matter

When it comes to black lives matter - you have some people who hate it, some people who love it, and some people like Sheriff David Clarke Jr. who think it's unnecessary. According to the Sheriff, there is no such thing as police brutality; however, contrary to that bold face lie – Americans have been well aware of police brutality even before it was publicized by the Rodney King video.

The fact is - White people, Black people, Asians, Latinos, Mexicans, ultimately - all nationalities have experienced some form of police brutality in this country. The problem a lot of people have with black lives matter is that they attached a color to the protest. It's not a secret that black people have been the victims of police brutality for decades. It's just now, since the creation of camera phones and social media – when it would have taken weeks or even months to make it to mainstream media - the videos now makes it to social media in seconds.

Truth is – no matter if you agree or disagree – black lives matter shined a light on a very serious problem that's been heavily ignored in this country – police brutality. Keyword in that sentence was *ignored*, because police brutality has never been unknown.

The FBI keeps stats on police brutality and on the nationalities of all victims. And believe it or not, white suspects are killed almost double the rate of black suspects. According to the Washington Post, in 2016 963 people died by the actions of police officers in this country; 233 victims were black and 465 victims were white, which is nearly double.

So how can police brutality be a racial problem? Even though in the mainstream media, it's painted as a white on black crime or a racially motivated incident, the reality is – the black lives matter movement protests police brutality no matter what nationality or race of the officer(s).

Protests are supposed to make people uncomfortable. And no one should expect that protesting the police should be easy. We should expect unrest and unease during a police protest. Believe it or not, it's in the best interest of the police to cause a riot during a police protest because it looks bad on the protestors, it validates the police's points, and it gives the police a reason to use excessive force which is the reason people are protesting in the first place.

How long are Americans supposed to sit back and watch the police act like the very same thugs they claim to be protecting us from? How long are Americans supposed to sit back and watch the media use excuses like black on black crime to justify an unlawful killing? I agree we might not like the protest, but it's necessary.

Because if black people don't protest police brutality, then who will? You can't get mad that black people protest police brutality, when white people are killed at almost double the rate and no one says anything.

Fact is – if the mainstream media covered police brutality on white suspects the same way they covered it on black suspects – we would be more aware of police brutality as a police problem and not as a racial problem, and definitely not as a black problem.

That's why people are screaming All Lives Matter; however, All Lives Matter is considered to be a watered down version Black Lives Matter, and in some cases a total disrespect to the black lives that were lost. I agree all lives do matter; however, the only time All Lives Matter chooses to protest is when a black life has been lost, not a white life or Latino life. So in reality, All Lives Matter is counterproductive and being used as a weapon to dilute the countless acts of violence being done by the police to black individuals.

So when people, like Joey Salads, hold up a sign that says "All Lives Matter" and then wonders why people are mad and then claims that Black Lives Matter is racist – it's not because black people think All Lives Don't Matter, it's because of the total and blatant disrespect of the black lives that were lost. Where was Joey Salads or All Lives Matter when Daniel Shaver, Hans Arellano, Brandon Ellingson, or Jerry Waller were gunned down by police? That's because All Lives Matter doesn't protest police brutality, it was created to dilute the message and protest the protesters.

On the other hand, Black Lives Matter needs to be more proactive in the defense of more than just black suspects. Because, if Black Lives Matter was truly an organization against police brutality, they would protest any unjustified use of excessive force – no matter the nationality of the victim(s).

However, Black Lives Matter has now been demonized and minimized down to a racist organization that is being used as a pawn in a George Soros conspiracy. And in my opinion, that's because there was no way of distinguishing the legit protesters from the dumb asses that showed up just to cause trouble. It doesn't help when the media tries to portray every act of violence and/or rioting as being done by a Black Lives Matter member, especially when there's not even an official membership.

Reality is - other than a hashtag, Black Lives Matter has no official leadership, no structure, no official logo, and not even an official spokesperson to denounce the bullshit and rioting. True, they have a website and it does list chapters across the country. But on the other hand, if you would've asked who was leading the Black Panther Party in the 60's and 70's, it was widely known from coast to coast without the internet or any websites. And when the media tried to portray the Black Panther Party as a racist organization, the leadership stood up, spoke up, and struck back saying loudly that they were not a racist organization. They announced that yes – they were against oppression and police brutality in the black community; however, they were willing to work with all races and nationalities to end oppression and police brutality as a whole.

Without official leadership, it didn't take long before the media, along with the help from a few dumbasses – to paint Black Lives Matter as a racist organization. And without any official leadership to refute the bullshit, it makes the motion of the movement that much more difficult. It also makes being able to work with and alongside other movements and organization damn near impossible.

Because as long as Americans continue to argue about which nationality or race the police is killing the most, constantly pointing the finger at one another – "WE" are not pointing the finger at the one problem that "WE" have in common, **THE POLICE**. Because police brutality is not a just Black problem, it's not just a White problem, and it's not just a Mexican or Latino problem. It's a TAXPAYERS problem.

If you don't think so, think about it this way. If the police unjustifiably beat and/or kill someone and then they get sued by the victim or victims' family in Civil Court, why are the TAXPAYERS financially responsible and not the Officer(s)?

The majority of the time it is because of the police union that Officers RARELY lose their jobs. So the reality is, "WE" as taxpayers are forced into continuing the employment of Officers who have "unjustifiably" assaulted and/or killed fellow taxpayers. These same Officers are then sued; they either lose or settle, which in turn, costs cities thousands and sometimes millions of dollars. Sometimes, they may have even been involved in multiple lawsuits throughout their career.

So like I said before police brutality is not a just Black problem, it's not just a White problem, and it's not just a Mexican or Latino problem.   It's a TAXPAYERS problem.

Message to Blue Lives Matter

Reality is, everyday Americans are losing trust in law enforcement. More and more often, Americans are seeing the videos and/or hearing about UNARMED CITIZENS being beaten, shot, or just flat out gunned downed by police officers. And yet somehow, some way, every homicide is justified.

Americans are tired of hearing about our teens being killed, our elderly being killed, our homeless being killed, our Veterans being killed, our mentally ill and/or handicap being killed - sometimes by the hands of the very same people we pay to protect us.

Every UNARMED shooting, every UNARMED beating, and every UNARMED death tears away more and more of the very little trust Americans have for law enforcement. That same very little trust is decreasing a little more and more every day - mainly because Officers have little to no accountability for their actions.

Sometimes, the entire investigation process and/or outcome is an insult to the American people. Why? Because our justice system relies on the testimony of good Officers but will take the testimony of **any** Officer. Even though it's no big secret that the police can lie too.

The sad reality of that is so many innocent Americans have had their vehicles searched, gotten tickets, paid fines, had their license suspended, served jail time, and/or have criminal records all due to the lies of a BAD OFFICER. Our justice system UNKNOWINGLY relies on the testimony of that bad Officer but never considers that Officer may not be telling the whole truth and nothing but the truth.

The problem is when Officers are caught falsifying evidence, caught falsifying arrests, caught committing perjury, caught committing police misconduct, or even caught in a unjustified killing of a citizen - our justice system does not go after Officers with the same vicious prosecution they would go after every other citizen.

For Example:

Marissa Alexander, a Florida woman who fired warning shots near her allegedly abusive husband, was sentenced to 20 years in prison, even though no one was harmed.

Compared to:

Reynaldo Goyos, the Officer who shot and killed Travis McNeil and wounded his friend Kareem Williams, as they sat in a car after a brief police chase. The shooting was only one of many in a string of deadly encounters between Miami Police Officers and black men. But it wasn't until Travis McNeil's death and the intense public outcry that the U.S. Department of Justice decided to investigate.

Believe it or not, Goyos was never prosecuted for the shooting. And it wasn't until two years later after a department Firearms Review Board ruled the shooting was "UNJUSTIFIED" that Goyos was fired. The Board said the evidence surrounding the shooting was inconsistent with Goyos' account of the event.

The arbitrator who reviewed the case, overturned Goyos' firing and ordered the department to return him to his job no later than August 13th of that year, with full back pay.

Where is the justice for the UNARMED victims who are beaten and/ or killed by police?

Where is the justice for the victims who are harassed, falsely accused, and/ or arrested by police?

Time after time, even when there's a clear dash cam video and audio proof of police misconduct, internal affairs RARELY finds any misconduct by officers.

Truth is – there is no such thing as justice when bad cops are being protected by bad cops.

And I truly believe there are good Officers with good intentions, but it seems that good Officers are stretched far and few.

We, as Americans, like to think the police officers role is to PROTECT US; unfortunately, the sad reality is that police departments are often more focused on making arrests and issuing citations because that's how they maintain and increase their funding. As a result of this, law enforcement agencies have outrageous budgets to maintain which means when crime is down, the budget is still the same. Regardless of what any law enforcement agencies say, they have to produce the numbers to maintain any level of funding.

This is what leads to overzealous Officers who fabricate charges, assault citizens, lie under oath, and only a few Officers, if any, face repercussions. But the BIGGEST issue that never gets addressed is that *some* police lie and our justice system believes they don't, which results in our justice system often receiving false information.

Not every incident leads to a public outcry but most peaceful protest are met with military style policing, armored vehicles, assault rifles, and chemical weapons like Tear Gas and industrial grade Mace.

This is not a third world country. This is America. But it seems as though THE POLICE HAVE DECLARED WAR ON THE AMERICAN PEOPLE on our own soil.

Message to the Super Americans

Patriotism is supporting the *Constitution*, not supporting the President. So if you feel like supporting Trump is more patriotic than supporting Obama, then you aren't really patriotic at all.

Reality is Trump's whole Inaugural speech was basically "American First" – buy American, hire American. A message that many people cheered for. However, that message came from a man that made millions, maybe billions from outsourcing – not hiring Americans. Flip a Trump product over and see if it says "Made in America". So how can he say claim to be putting America first?

Patriotism is supporting the proper policies, not people. Patriotism is supporting the right laws and legislation, not supporting the unconstitutional executive orders. Like Trumps illegal "Muslim Ban", excuse me, his so-called "Travel Ban". Because unless you're a Native American Indian – your ancestor weren't born in the United States. It's sad to say, even in 2017, some Americans will sit by and watch the government, along with the oil companies, basically bully and steal the Native American's scared land and possibly contaminate their water supply.

Funny thing is – when you compare a story like the Keystone Pipeline to the Bundy Standoff, the Americans standing their ground against a big oil company were considered protestors. And all the Americans that showed up with firearms to support Cliven Bundy were considered patriots. What's the difference? The Native Americans were protecting their scared land and water supply while Cliven Bundy was in an armed standoff over **federal land**.

Super Americans are the Americans who are not afraid to stand up against unconstitutional practices. For example, the hundreds of thousands of Americans who showed up at airports across the United States to protest Trump's unconstitutional travel ban and supported those who were being illegally detained.

Frankly, I'm tired of people saying that protesting is un-American. Protesting is our American right and

Freedom of Speech is part of our First Amendment and foundation of our country. People need stop acting like the core foundation of America is ONLY the Second Amendment – being an American is more than the Right to Bear Arms. Being American is more than flying a flag and fireworks on the 4th. So quit saying people are un-American if they don't believe what you believe, if they don't see society the way you see it or if they don't vote the way you voted.

Because right now the country is being run by a baby tyrant. And it's up to the real patriots, who value the constitution and this country to investigate, expose, to hold Trump accountable, and hopefully impeach him.

This can be accomplished with strong political minds and strong political voices who are not afraid to call "*bullshit*" and expose Trump for his lies, false claims, and his continuous misuse of his position for financial gain.

Message to the Mainstream News Media

Mainstream Media and Politics

When it comes to crime and politics, the mainstreams media is supposed to give it to the public straight. Reality is – we get 20% truth and 80% lies – depending on who the story is about or who is telling the story. That's why so many people are screaming Fake News! They way stories are reported are biased depending on which news channel you watch. Frankly, the media is too busy beefing against each other to give a complete story. Often, the media ends up making the story more inflammatory than necessary or engaging in the overall cover up. Especially when it comes to politics and especially when it comes to Trump. News outlets like CNN, MSNBC, ABC, and the Washington Post more than often create drama out of minor stories, over exaggerate facts, and sometimes seem like they're in full Trump attack mode. On the other hand FOX minus a few news anchors are too busy brown nosing Trumps orange ass to report any facts that paint Trump in a negative light – overall misleading their viewers by presenting Trump as the "victim". To be honest about it, host like Bill O'Reilly, Sean Hannity, Tucker Carson would rather disregard the truth, make excuses, or attack the facts than call Trump out on his bullshit and lies. That's why so many people are turning independent news sources like the Young Turks, Democracy Now, and even YouTubers like Phillip DeFranco or Jesse Dollemore – because they don't employ or pay for political surrogates to give their one sided opinions.

Mainstream Media and Police Brutality

When it comes to police brutality, it is NEVER reported equally. Many times, if the suspect is black, we know more about his past crimes than the crime they were being assaulted or killed for. How often does the mainstream media ever report police brutality on a white suspect, even though the FBI stats clearly state more unarmed white suspects are killed by law enforcement than black suspects? Why isn't police brutality on white suspects' mainstream media – especially when some cases are far more heinous than Tamir Rice and Philando Castile cases? For example, the case of Daniel Shaver, an unarmed white man shot to death while complying by crawling on the floor to the police. Is it because if you report on white suspects just like you report on the black suspects – maybe you will expose the police brutality for what it really is?

Instead – news outlets hire people like Sheriff David Clarke, Jr. to make excuses, point fingers and play the blame game. Police brutality is real. So why would the news media outlets allow Clarke to pedal his insane theory that there is no such thing as police brutality in the United States?

Is it because he's black? And news outlets needed a black face to say it was ok for black people to be dying by the hands of police? Because cases like Tamir Rice, Philando Castile, and Sandra Bland show that police brutality is alive and kicking.

As much as I wish it wasn't true, the same thing goes for when the police are attacked by suspects. Every time an officer is attacked by a black suspect – it makes national headlines, but it rarely makes any headline when an officer is attacked by a white suspect. For example, the two Officers in Iowa who were ambushed and killed by Scott M. Greene barely made local news.

Truth is – the media is so biased it doesn't even know it's biased. Majority of the time – you can tell the nationality of the suspect just by the title of the story. Because if he's anything other than white – it's mentioned in the title. Not to mention, the media linking every attack in America to radical Islam or ISIS and not calling American Christian terror attacks exactly what they are. Dylan Roof was a terrorist and committed an act of terrorism to start a race war, but he was NEVER called a terrorist by the mainstream media, yet they did report on him being taken to Burger King by the arresting officers.

It's not all your fault because the majority of the time you're just reporting the half-facts and half-truths you receive, but it is your fault on how you report it.

It's your fault when you allow the police to fudge the facts to paint their victims as vicious suspects while you – the media disregards the vicious attack on the suspect. It's your fault when you choose to look more into the suspects' background other than the Officer(s) that were accused of excessive force. It's your fault when you choose to display the worst possible photo of a black suspect but show the graduation photo of a white suspect.

In my opinion the mainstream media is solely to blame for racial division in this country, because it is you who chooses to paint black communities and black suspects as violent and white communities as victims and white suspects as mentally disturbed, lone wolfs, or misunderstood.

But what should we expect when this country is more than 60% white and the media is designed to keep Americans in fear? If the media reported white on white crime or any heinous crime committed by a white suspect, it wouldn't strike fear in the hearts and minds of the masses. This country was built on racial division so reporting on racial incidents is what draws in the ratings. So it doesn't matter if the incident wasn't racially motivated - it's always reported to imply it. That's what fuels the racial division in this country.

Add in the fact that the mainstream media chooses to report only on black suspects of police violence like Tamir Rice, Phalndo Castile, Sandra Bland, and Eric Gardner – and not the cases of white suspects like Daniel Shaver, Hans Arellano, Brandon Ellingson, or Jerry Waller.

Why? Because it doesn't fit the narrative. It's easier to make the masses afraid of people who look different than them. It's easier to publicly convict a person of color when your whole narrative revolves around demonizing people of color. And I use the word demonizing because if a black suspect is shot and/or killed by a police officer, the media intentionally displays as much negativity about the suspect as humanly possible, almost subconsciously justifying the Officers' actions. When in fact, in most cases, the accused Officer has had numerous infractions that the public rarely hears about.

Biased much?

According to the mainstream media, the news is supposed to be an independent source, but from where I'm standing the news was designed to cause racial division, fear, unrest, and unease in this country.

Truth is, it's very rare to see what I like to call a "feel good" story and it's not because they don't exist. It's because those stories don't get the same amount of ratings as an immigrant fear mongering story or a story with a catchy title like "Welfare Queen". Just like stories about white kids rioting during pumpkin fest, flipping over cars, and setting cars on fire – they don't bring in the same ratings as another Chicago black on black crime story.

If you don't think the mainstream media is designed to portray people of color, especially black men, as violent and uneducated - then ask yourself this, why does the mainstream media always report on Chicago's black on black crime, yet they neglect to report that for the last 7 years - 100% of the graduates from Urban Prep Academy, an all-black all-male high school – were accepted into a 4 year college or university? It's because it doesn't fit the narrative of a city out of control and it doesn't get the ratings. Police brutality is about ratings and ratings only matter to news outlets.

Because if the news media truly wanted to report on the impact that police brutality has on society as a whole, they would report on white victims equally as black victims. They would report on the millions and millions of dollars that police brutality cost each and every city or how taxpayers pick up the tab for lawsuits, judgements, and settlements.

To be honest about it, there is no such thing as unbiased news when it comes to police brutality, all news organizations care about is RATINGS, RATNGS, RATINGS, not about Americans, not about justice, and definitely not about the victims.

Message to the Justice System

When it comes to the amount of crime in this country, no one will dispute that criminals deserve to be punished. However, when you look at our justice system and the judgments that are handed out, it makes you take a step back to re-evaluate what justice really is and if the justice system has been tainted.

Let's be real about it, there is no shortage of corruption in our justice system, nor is there a shortage in wrongful convictions, and even wrongful executions. And with America leading the World in mass incarcerations, how can we turn a blind eye to a system that seems to be broken beyond repair? Think about it, this is a country where politicians make promises to fight the never-ending war on drugs, not promises to fight the war on poverty and drug addiction.

Not only that, we live in a country where politicians run campaigns with the promise to be tough on crime, and believe it or not, we live in a country where states have signed contracts with privately owned prisons to keep them more than 70% occupied.

Makes you wonder who the lawmakers really serve? And makes you wonder how our public officials can really serve us when they are contractually obligated to private prison and their quotas?

Think about it, this is a country where Management & Training Corp. threatened to sue the state of Arizona because a line in their contract guaranteed that the prison would remain 97% full. Management & Training Corp. even had the nerve to argue that they lost nearly $10 million from the reduction in inmate population. And guess what, the state of Arizona settled, paying Management & Training Corp. $3 million for empty beds.

No – let's keep it real, the state of Arizona paid $3 million dollars in taxpayer's money for the reduction in crime, money that could've been spent on schools, roads, or even drug addiction.

The problem doesn't start with private prison; it starts with the judges and the lawyers. And even though the

6th amendment gives defendants the right to counsel, adequate defense is determined between those who can or cannot pay.

Reality is, public defenders are over worked and underpaid so they have no interest in actually fighting a case. The majority of the time they would rather counsel defendants toward a plea. Not to mention that most district attorneys and prosecutors are more concerned with getting another notch under their belt and ultimately becoming a judge, rather than being concerned with the actual truth.

Let's be honest, prosecutors are arguably some of the most powerful people in the American justice system;

however, that same justice system is not equipped and sometimes not even willing to punish prosecutors for their crimes. Reality is, the victims of prosecutorial misconduct rarely see justice and the result is innocent people serve time and sometimes lose their life because a prosecutor(s) are trying to make a name for themselves.

Combine that with the fact that defense attorneys, prosecutors, judges, and sometimes police officers form relationships and friendships with each other. Friendships and relationships that are formed in the best interest of their careers and not in the best interest of the people that they represent or the citizens they serve. And in situations like that, the rules of law are obsolete and there is no such thing as innocent until proven guilty nor is there such thing as the burden of proof. So for their victims – there is no such thing as *justice*.

Honestly, how can justice even be considered justice when prosecutors allow witnesses to perjure themselves with no repercussions? How can justice even be considered justice when prosecutors suppress evidence just to get a win?

Think about it, how can justice even be considered justice when prosecutors and lawyers are making backroom deals by trading wins and losses to further their careers? How can justice even be considered justice when district attorneys and judges receive campaign donations and, in some cases, financial kickbacks from private prison corporations?

Truth is, there can't be justice in a system that is openly corrupt, and undeniably broken.

However, in my opinion the system isn't broken; it's fixed, better yet rigged. Rigged in favor of the haves and biased against the have nots. Rigged to financially benefit private prisons.

As Americans, we want to believe that none of that is true. We want to believe the justice system in this country is fair and just. However, it's not. And the facts prove fairness, or should I say so called "justice" in this country, is one sided.

If you don't think justice is one sided, then ask yourself this, how can Ethan Couch steal alcohol, then kill four people in a DUI crash, and then only get sentenced to serve six months for each person he killed?

If you don't think justice is one sided, then ask yourself this, how can Brock Turner get sentenced to only 6 months in jail for sexually assaulting an unconscious female student? While people like Timothy Jackson and Ronald Washington are sentenced to life without parole for theft of less than $200?

If you don't think justice is one sided, then ask yourself why so many young Blacks and Latinos are sentenced to years behind bars for the nonviolent crimes of possession, while white kids are basically given a slap on the wrist?

Is this what our justice system calls justice? Basically letting murders and rapists go free, while using the full force of the law to prosecute nonviolent offenders? That's justice?

The facts don't lie, nor do the numbers. And when the American Civil Liberties Union (ACLU) conducted a study in 2013, they found out that more than 3,200 people who are serving life sentences, without the possibility of parole, are serving these sentences for nonviolent offenses. And it should come as no surprise that 65% are African American, 18% are white, and 16% are Latino – evidence of what the ACLU calls "extreme racial disparities" and what some people call the new Jim Crow or slavery by a different name.

However, America will never acknowledge slavery has moved away from the cotton fields to behind the prison walls. Nor will America ever acknowledge that prison is no longer about rehabilitation and more about maximizing profits from cheap labor.

Let's be real about it, companies like UNICOR line up to take advantage of the cheap *slave* labor. Honestly, why would they want to pay people minimum wage when they can pay prisoners less than a $1 an hour or as low as $0.16 an hour for that same position?

Let's be honest, the American justice system is only concerned with locking individuals up, making them live in less than humane living conditions, forcing them to work for slave wages, and never offering them any form of rehabilitation.

Sounds like slavery to me, but that is what our justice system calls "justice".

Message to Americans

It's our responsibility to remain patriotic and not let our personal views, personal beliefs, or political party to tear apart our Country or undermine the basic fundamentals of our Constitution.

It's our responsibility to not let politics and the mainstream media side track us with their tactics of racial division.

Because as long as I'm blaming you and you're blaming me – we're not blaming them.

Dedicated

"To all the lives lost due to police violence and systematic injustice."